Re

Englisn idioms

D'Arcy Vallance

Illustrator: Anthony Maher
Editors: Andy Hopkins and
Joc Potter

Books for Learners

Contents

6

Introduction

What is an idiom?

An idiom is a phrase with a special meaning. For example, *'I was over the moon'* means 'I was very pleased and excited.' *'I was pulling your leg'* means 'I was joking when I said that.'

  When you see or hear an idiom, you may know all the words in it (*moon, pull, leg* etc.) but you may not know what the idiom means.

Why are idioms useful?

In spoken English, idioms are used in most situations, from social conversations to business meetings. In written English, they are especially common in news stories because the writers want to make the news interesting and lively.

What will I learn from this book?

You will learn idioms from modern everyday English. They are presented in short, entertaining texts and funny cartoons. At the end, there's also an alphabetical list with more examples.

How to use the book

Enjoy the texts and cartoons, learning as you read. Each text contains three or four idioms in **bold letters**. Definitions below each text help you to check your understanding.

At the end of each chapter, short review questions help you remember what you have learned. Answers are at the back of the book.

Read - Enjoy - Learn

1
People

Types of people

Does it matter if someone says you're **no rocket scientist**? Yes, it does! This phrase means *not very intelligent*.
What if a newspaper describes a politician as a **dark horse**? This means nobody knows much about him.
And a **party pooper**? This means a person who spoils enjoyable activities by refusing to join in. This idiom is also useful in apologies: *'I'm sorry to be a party pooper, but I have to go home now.'*

no rocket scientist
not very intelligent person

dark horse
secretive person

party pooper
person who spoils fun

*He was **no rocket scientist** with computers.*

Brains and beauty

A Hollywood actress once met the British philosopher, Bertrand Russell. Whereas he was quite ugly, she **turned heads** wherever she went. She was rather **full of herself** and said to Russell, 'They say I'm the most beautiful woman in the world, and I hear you're the smartest man. Imagine if we had a child with your brains and my beauty.'

Russell, who was never **lost for words**, replied, 'Imagine if it had my beauty and your brains.'

turn heads
attract a lot of attention

full of yourself
too pleased with yourself

lost for words
not knowing what to say

12

*Her car **turned** almost as many **heads**
as she did.*

Larger than life

Say 'Sean Connery' to **the man in the street** and he'll probably say 'James Bond'. The famous British secret agent, 007, has been played by seven film actors in the last forty years, but Connery was the original and probably the best. He was **larger than life** both on the screen and **in the flesh**. Even in his 60s, he was chosen by the readers of an international women's magazine as The World's Most Attractive Man.

the man in the street
an average person

larger than life
more exciting than normal

in the flesh
as a real person

*James Bond, the **larger-than-life** secret agent, was first played by Sean Connery.*

Twins

Some twins are identical, but my brother and I are definitely not. He's a **couch potato** who watches television all weekend and thinks exercise is a **dirty word**, whereas I'm always **on the go**, playing sport, socialising, working and so on. He says I'm a **pain in the neck** because I never stop doing things and making a noise while he's trying to watch the TV or sleep.

couch potato
lazy person who watches a lot of TV

dirty word
something unpleasant

on the go
active

pain in the neck
annoying nuisance (person or thing)

A **couch** is any long comfortable piece of furniture to sit on, such as a sofa.

Review 1

Answers at the back >

A Match the idioms and meanings.

1 larger than life   a) obscure person

2 dark horse   b) exciting

3 on the go   c) active, busy

B Complete the idioms.

1 She was so surprised that she was lost
    .... .

2 He's too full .... to be interested in us.

3 My little brother can be a pain .....

4 The man in .... cares more about money
   than politics.

C Think about real people ...

1 Is there a couch potato in your family?

2 Do you know someone who turns
   heads?

3 Have you ever met a film star in the
   flesh?

4 Have you ever been a party pooper?

2

Emotions

All kinds

Anger, happiness, love, hate, fear, boredom - whatever you feel, there's an idiom to put it into words. And if something doesn't excite you at all, you can say, 'It **leaves me cold**.' You can express moderate feelings such as 'I'm **on edge'** - as you might feel before making a speech or having a tooth out - or strong feelings such as 'I was **bored to death / worried to death / scared to death**.'

leaves me cold
has no effect on me

on edge
anxious

(-ed) to death
extremely (-ed)

*I'm sorry, Charles, but orchestral music just **leaves me cold**.*

Laughter

Somebody told a very funny joke at the
office yesterday, and we were all **in
stitches** for five minutes afterwards. Then
the boss came in. He was in a bad mood
and started to talk about a work problem.
I couldn't forget the joke and I couldn't
keep a straight face. The boss asked me
what I was smiling at. When I told him,
he just looked at me and said nothing. I
thought he was going to throw me out.
But then he **burst out laughing**!

in stitches
laughing a lot and unable to stop

keep a straight face
avoid smiling or laughing

burst out laughing
suddenly laugh loudly

*Everyone was **in stitches***.

Happiness

It's a beautiful day, and I feel **on top of the world**!

He's just had some good news. He's got the job that he wanted, and he's **over the moon** about it.

Getting my first job as an actor was so exciting. I was **on cloud nine** for weeks afterwards.

on top of the world
in a very happy mood

over the moon
very excited and pleased about something

on cloud nine
very happy about something for a continuing period

*He was **over the moon**.*

Road rage

rage = violent anger

As roads become busier, road rage is becoming more common. Ben Smith, 43, from London, was trying to park his car yesterday when another driver got in first. Smith **saw red**, jumped out, shouted at the other driver and started kicking the man's car, doing £800 worth of damage. Smith told police later, 'I don't know **what got into** me. I've never done anything like that before. I just **lost it**.'

see red
suddenly feel extreme anger

what got into him
why he became so extreme

lost it
lost control

***What's got into** him?*

Broken heart

Almost as soon as he met her,
he fell **head over heels** in love with
her. They had six wonderful months
together, and then she left him.
It **broke his heart**,
and now a year later
he's only just
beginning to
pick up the pieces.

head over heels
suddenly very much in love

break someone's heart
make someone very sad

pick up the pieces
rebuild something that was damaged

28

She **broke his heart** when she said
goodbye.

Review 2

Answers at the back >

A Match the idioms and meanings.

1 on edge   a) laughing a lot

2 in stitches   b) feel very angry

3 lose it   c) anxious

4 see red   d) be out of control

B Complete the idioms.

1 I feel on top .... when the sun shines.

2 She burst .... when she saw me.

3 I'm on cloud .... whenever we're together.

4 He suddenly hit me. I don't know what .... him.

C Can you remember a time when you

1 were scared to death?

2 saw a film that left you cold?

3 couldn't keep a straight face?

4 were over the moon about something?

30

3

Social relations

Party!

January **6**

*I went to a big party last night. The hosts were celebrating something so they'd decided to **push the boat out**: there was a really good band, fantastic food and lots of drink. I chatted to a few people for the first hour - just the usual **small talk**. Then I met this great guy. We got talking and we really **hit it off**. I'm seeing him tomorrow!*

push the boat out

spend more than usual on something

small talk

polite conversation about unimportant things

hit it off

like each other at a first meeting

*They really **pushed the boat out** for their daughter's wedding.*

A good friend

A good friend is someone who

- will always **be there for** you when you need them.
- **sees eye to eye** with you about most things.
- is not perfect and not the same as you, but is good at **give and take**.

be there for
be ready to help

see eye to eye
agree about things

give and take
compromise and cooperation

*Even best friends don't **see eye to eye** about everything.*

What to say

How can you say '*No*' to an invitation for now but keep the invitation open for another time?

• *Can I **take a rain check**?*

What can you say if someone invites you to an event that is dependent on something else, such as good weather.

• *(Let's keep our) **fingers crossed**.*

And if someone offers to pay for drinks or a meal, but you want to pay for him/her?

• *This is **on me**.*

take a rain check
keep an invitation open

fingers crossed
Let's hope for the best.

It's on me / him.
I'll pay. / He'll pay.

*The dinner's **on me**.*

a rain check comes from the US: a rain check is
a ticket for later use. It's given to spectators when
a sports event can't go ahead because of rain.

People at work

Old Mr Brown has been with the company for years. He's pretty useless, but he survives because the manager **has a soft spot** for him.

There are two bossy middle-aged women who are always **at each other's throats** about one thing or another.

And there's a nice girl who started last week and is **a breath of fresh air**.

have a soft spot for
like, care about

at each other's throats
arguing

breath of fresh air
pleasantly different

The new young secretary
Is a breath of fresh air.

Review 3

A Match the idioms and meanings.

1 see eye to eye   a) like each other
2 it's on me   b) Let's hope
3 hit it off   c) I'll pay
4 fingers crossed   d) agree

B Complete the idioms.

1 The nice new secretary was a breath ....
2 You paid last time. This meal is ....
3 I think he has a .... for you.
4 Thanks, but I can't come tonight. Can I
   take a ....?
5 Give and .... is important in a good
   relationship.

C Think about your social life:

1 Are you good at small talk?
2 Do you try to be there for your friends?
3 When did you last push the boat out?

4
Dating
and
Romance

She likes me.

TOM: I think she likes me.

SAM: **In your dreams**!

TOM: No, really, I'm sure she does.

SAM: **No way**! She never even looks at you.

TOM: Exactly! That means one of two things: either she's embarrassed because she fancies me, or she's **playing hard to get**.

SAM: Tom, there is a third possibility ...

In your dreams.
it's a very unrealistic hope

no way
definitely not

play hard to get
pretend to be uninterested

43

Gossip

ETHEL: Have you heard about Jane's
        boyfriend?

MAVIS: The one she's been **going steady**
        with for about six months?

ETHEL: No. **He's history**. She's got a
        new one.

MAVIS: That's fast!

ETHEL: Yes. And he's younger than
        her! - Oh! Hello, Jane.

JANE: Haven't you got anything better
        to do than gossip about other
        people? **Get a life**!

going steady
in a regular relationship

he/she's history
past, not important now

get a life
do something interesting (not polite)

*No, **he's history**.*
She's got a new
boyfriend.

Drop-dead gorgeous

Dear Romance Magazine

My boyfriend is **drop-dead gorgeous**, kind and sensitive, and we have a great relationship. He's also very tall. (I **have a thing about** tall men, so that's important to me too!) The problem is that I want to get married and have children, but he doesn't. I love him, but he's never going to **pop the question**. What should I do?

Julie (London)

drop-dead gorgeous
very attractive

have a thing about
react strongly to / like/dislike very much

pop the question
ask 'Will you marry me?'

*Everyone thinks he's **drop-dead gorgeous**.*

Love at first sight

There's a romantic story about the nineteenth-century Italian revolutionary, Garibaldi. He was on his ship entering a port when he saw a beautiful woman standing on the shore. 'That's the woman I'm going to marry,' he said. It was **love at first sight**. The woman, when she met him, was **swept off her feet** by his good looks and personality. They were married within days and **only had eyes for** each other for the rest of their lives.

love at first sight
falling in love immediately

sweep someone off their feet
make them fall in love quickly

only have eyes for
only be interested in

It was **love at first sight**.

Dating dilemma

On a first date, who should pay for meals, drinks, tickets etc.? In the old days, the man would **pick up the tab**, but nowadays nobody is quite sure. Will the woman think he's a dinosaur if he pays? Or will she think he's mean if he doesn't? Will the man be grateful if the woman suggests they **go Dutch** or will he be insulted? There's no right answer. You just have to **play it by ear**. Be sensitive to your partner's feelings and you'll probably get it right.

pick up the tab
pay the total

go Dutch
share the cost of a meal or entertainment

play it by ear
not follow a plan

*Do you fancy **going Dutch**?*

Review 4

A Match the idioms and meanings.

1 no way   a) share costs
2 go steady   b) definitely not
3 he's history   c) in a regular
4 go Dutch   relationship
                d) in the past

B Complete the idioms.

1 As soon as they met, it was love .... .
2 He took out a ring and popped .... .
3 Some people plan, others play it .... .
4 He's in love and only has .... for her.

C Do you know someone who

1 is drop-dead gorgeous?
2 plays hard to get?
3 never picks up the tab?

D Complete the idioms on this and the next page.

1

MAN: *Come and have a drink with me.*

WOMAN: ***In*** *........................ !"*

All Andy's girlfriends have had ponytails.
*I guess he **has a** .... ponytails.*

5

Life
situations

Lottie's diary

January **7**

*I've just finished reading 'Bridget
Jones's Diary' by Helen Fielding
today. It's a very popular book, and I
really loved it because Bridget and I
are **in the same boat**: we're both
looking for **Mr Right** (without
success) and trying to do well in our
careers (without success), and we're
both sure that we'll get there as soon
as we can lose weight, get fit and
generally **get our act together**.*

in the same boat
in the same situation

Mr Right
the right man to marry

get your act together
get organised and prepared

*You'll find **Mr Right***
  one day, dear.

In hot water

MIKE: Tom's **in hot water**.

JAKE: Why? What's he done?

MIKE: He borrowed a company car without permission and smashed it up.

JAKE: Is he OK?

MIKE: Yes, he's fine, but I wouldn't like to be **in his shoes** when the boss finds out.

JAKE: Oh, he'll make up a good story and get **off the hook**. He always does.

in hot water
in trouble

in your shoes
in your situation

off the hook
out of trouble

Country life

After five years of **life in the fast lane**, Janie decided to give up her well-paid city job and start a new life in a small country village. But although she was pleased to escape from **the rat race**, she was **a fish out of water** in the country. Now she's back in the city, wiser for her experience.

life in the fast lane
fast, high-pressure lifestyle

rat race
competitive working life

a fish out of water
uncomfortable in a strange situation

She was pleased to escape
*from **the rat race**.*

Team on a roll

England on a roll

After a difficult start to the competition, when England did well to **keep their heads above water** in the match against the strong Brazilian team (result: 1-1), the England team have been **on a roll -** winning every match including last night's spectacular game which ended in a 3-0 win. However, they can't afford to **put their feet up** because the next match will be the hardest yet.

keep your head above water
survive

on a roll
enjoying continual success

put your feet up
relax

The England team made the mistake of
***putting their feet up** too early.*

Review 5

A Match the idioms and meanings.

1 Mr Right   a) relax
2 hot water   b) trouble
3 put my feet up   c) the ideal husband
4 off the hook   d) out of trouble

B Complete the idioms.

1 We're in the same .... , so let's help
   each other.
2 You need to get your .... together and
   find a job.
3 He left the rat .... to do charity work.
4 How would you feel if you were in my
   .... ?

C Which of these is not enjoyable?

1 putting your feet up
2 feeling like a fish out of water
3 being on a roll

6

Conversation

A film scene

In the film *Four Weddings and a Funeral*, Hugh Grant meets an old friend, and asks him, 'How are you, and how's your girlfriend?'

The man replies, 'She's not my girlfriend anymore.'

'That's good,' says Grant, 'You probably didn't know, but she was **two-timing** you with someone else.'

The man looks deeply shocked and says, 'She's my *wife* now.'

Hugh Grant realises he has **put his foot in it**. He **kicks himself** for being stupid.

two-timing
deceiving, being unfaithful

put your foot in it
unintentionally upset someone

kick yourself
feel angry with yourself

Hugh Grant realises he has
put his foot in it.

Can you keep a secret?

A friend has just told you a secret. Then someone asks, 'What were you two talking about?'

Do you -

(a) smile and just say mysteriously, '**That would be telling**'?

(b) **spill the beans**?

Your friends are planning a surprise party for someone.

Do you –

(a) keep your mouth shut until the party?

(b) **let the cat out of the bag** the day before?

That would be telling.
it's a secret

spill the beans
reveal a secret

let the cat out of the bag
give secret information too early

*Don't **let the cat out of the bag**.*

Opinions

Is **B** agreeing or disagreeing?

A: He talks too much.
B: **You're telling *me***! I sat next to him on the bus yesterday!

A: It's hot today, isn't it?
B: **You can say *that* again**.

A: He's an intelligent boy; the real problem is that he's lazy.
B: I think you've **hit the nail on the head**.

You're telling *me*.
I know that (even better than you)

You can say *that* again.
I agree strongly

hit the nail on the head
describe something accurately

Believe me!

SAM: Hello?

TOM: Sam! Help me!

SAM: What's the matter, Tom?

TOM: I'm hanging from this rock by one hand. I can't hold on much longer. Call the rescue service quickly!

SAM: Very funny, Tom. Why are you always **pulling my leg**?

TOM: Sam! I'm not **having you on**. It's true! Honestly!

SAM: **Pull the other one**, Tom!

pull someone's leg
play a (friendly) trick on someone

have someone *on*
say something untrue (usually for fun)

pull the *other* one
I don't believe you. I can see your trick

*I'M NOT **PULLING YOUR LEG**!!*

Hot ears

Have you heard this joke?

A: My ears got burnt!

B: How?

A: I was ironing when the phone rang. Instead of picking up the phone I picked up the iron.

B: That must've hurt!

A: **To say the least**.

B: Let's **get this straight**: you said you burnt both ears. Right?

A: Yes.

B: How **on Earth** did you burn the other ear?

A: The person called again.

to say the least
very much

get it straight
be clear about it

on Earth
I can't imagine

*It was uncomfortable, **to say the least**.*

Review 6

A Match the idioms and meanings.

1 two-time   a) reveal a secret
2 spill the beans   b) be unfaithful
3 You're telling   c) teasing me
   me.   d) I know that already
4 pulling my leg   and I agree

B Complete the idioms.

1   A: Look! A spider behind you!
     B: Pull .... .

2   A: What's the secret?
     B: That would .... .

3   A: This is difficult.
     B: You can say .... .

4   A: Is this cheese from Spain?
     B: Yes. You've hit .... .

C For *you*, which feels the worst?

1 kicking yourself for forgetting
   something important
2 putting your foot in it
3 realising that someone is having you on
4 letting the cat out of the bag by mistake

76

7

Thinking
and
learning

Predictions

Who is the most optimistic person? Who is the most pessimistic?

CHRIS: I think we might get a good pay rise this year.

SAM: **That'll be the day**!

TOM: I think it's **on the cards**.

HELEN: I think it's **a safe bet**. The company's made a big profit.

KATE: You're right, but it's still **touch and go** whether they'll share it with us.

That'll be the day.
That will be worth celebrating (said ironically – it will never really happen)

on the cards (*in* **the cards** - US English)
likely

a safe bet
almost certain / can be relied on

touch and go
very unsure

*I thought you said he was **a safe bet**.*

Memory

A woman was having dinner with an elderly friend and the friend's husband. She noticed that her friend always called her husband loving names like 'Honey', 'Darling', 'Sweetheart' etc.

While the husband was out of the room, the woman said, 'It's 70 years since you two **tied the knot**, but you still call him those pet names. That's wonderful! It must **take some doing** to keep romance alive for so long.'

Her friend answered, 'The truth is that his name **slipped my mind** about ten years ago.'

tie the knot
get married

take some doing
not be easy

slip your mind
disappear from your memory

*He suddenly realised that the speaker's name had **slipped his mind**.*

Pronunciation

A **golden rule** of pronunciation is: use word stress correctly.

You probably know that one part of a word is 'stressed' (= stronger than the other parts), for example: PHOtograph, phoTOgrapher, photoGRAPHic.

Listen for the stress in words. Then you'll **get the hang of** word stress and be able to use it more correctly. If you can do this, your pronunciation will improve **just like that**.

golden rule
important rule

get the hang of
learn how to do or use something

just like that
quickly and easily

*Boris thought he was **getting the hang of** the language until he tried ordering a cup of coffee.*

Listening

Learners of English sometimes say, 'I don't listen to English on the radio because it's too fast and I **can't make head nor tail of** it.

But think about that. When you were a few months old, learning your own language **from scratch**, did you understand it all? No! But you listened and learned. Then you learned to speak and read and write. But listening came first. So even if you don't feel confident, **have a go** at it.

can't make head nor tail of
can't understand

from scratch
from the beginning

have a go
have a try

I can't make
head nor tail of *it.*

Fear of flying

Statistics prove that flying is a very safe method of transport, but this **cut no ice** with Jean Fellows, 60, and nobody could persuade her to try to overcome her lifelong fear. That was until her seven-year-old granddaughter told her to be brave and try.

It is unusual for the words of a child to **carry** more **weight** than those of adults, but Jean **took them to heart** and finally bought an air ticket. 'It wasn't as bad as I thought,' she said after the flight.

cut no ice
have no influence

carry weight
have influence

take to heart
consider seriously

*The steward's attempt to calm the passengers would have **carried** more **weight** if he had removed his parachute*

Review 7

A Match the idioms and meanings.

1 touch and go   a) unsure
2 on the cards   b) get married
3 tie the knot   c) try
4 have a go   d) likely

B Complete the idioms.

1 We'll have to start again from ....

2 Some people can memorise phrases just ....

3 A golden .... of learning is to practise   regularly.

4 It's a safe .... that I'll forget some of these   idioms.

5 I couldn't swim at the beginning of the course but now I'm getting ....

C Look at the pictures on the next two pages and complete the idioms.

1

MOTHER: Is your room clean and tidy?

FATHER: Ha ha! That'll be .... !

*I don't understand adults. I explained that
I couldn't do the homework because of an
important party last night, but it cut
.... with him at all.*

8
Action

Sleepy burglar

This is a true story about a French burglar. After getting into an empty house easily through an open window, he probably thought his job was **a piece of cake**. He decided to **take his time** and went into the kitchen, where he found some champagne. After drinking the whole bottle, he went to look for jewellery in the bedroom but fell asleep on the bed. He didn't wake up until the owners returned, **catching him red handed**.

piece of cake
very easy

take your time
don't hurry

catch someone red handed
catch someone doing something bad

*He was **caught red handed** when the owners came home.*

Action hero

Action movie heroes may seem strong and independent, but they have to follow rules:

1 Never do things **by the book**. Forget about correct procedures.
2 Always wait till the last possible moment before **turning the tables** on the bad guys.
3 When you're **in the thick of** the action, your hair and make-up still have to look good.

by the book
following the rules

turn the tables
reverse the situation

in the thick of
in the most active part

*Action heroes have to look good **in the thick of** the action.*

Sports idioms

From British football:

The government has scored **an own goal** by reducing tax at a time when it needs extra money.

From American baseball:

It would be nice to exchange news. Let's **touch base** next week.

From boxing:

The gloves are off in this political campaign, with both candidates using personal attacks and dirty tricks.

an own goal
something that harms you and not your opponent

touch base
get/keep in contact briefly

The gloves are off
The fight is very aggressive.

96

*An **own goal***

Losing weight

January **9**

Today was going to be the day that I started to lose weight. Well, I went for a run in the park with Victoria. I thought that would **do the trick**, but it nearly killed me. She kept looking back and telling me to **step on it**. It's no good. I've left it too late. Once you're over 30, you've **missed the boat**. I'm just going to get fat and enjoy it. Now, where are those chocolates that I threw away?

do the trick
be the way to solve the problem

step *on* it
go faster (like stepping on a car's accelerator pedal)

miss the boat
be too late

Come on!
*Let's **step on it!***

Job on the line

Bill had a problem waking up in the mornings. One day his boss said angrily, 'You're late for work every day. You probably think I'm **a soft touch**, but I'm not, and your job's **on the line**.'

So Bill went to his doctor, who gave him a pill, which Bill took before he went to bed. He slept much better than usual and woke up early. Arriving at work, he said, 'Boss, I'm **on top of** the problem!'

'That's fine,' said the boss, 'but where were you yesterday?'

soft touch
easy to get things from

on the line
at risk

on top of
in control of

*Your job's **on the line** if you can't **get on top of** this problem.*

Review 8

A Match the idioms and meanings.

1 piece of cake	a) go faster
2 take your time	b) easy
3 step on it	c) don't hurry
4 miss the boat	d) be too late

B Complete the idioms.

1 The police caught the thief red .... .

2 The campaign has started, and the gloves .... .

3 We made a mistake and scored .... .

4 The doctor said, 'These pills will do ...

C Can you think of a film in which -

1 a police officer doesn't do things by the book?

2 the hero turns the tables on the bad guys?

3 the hero is always in the thick of the action but is never hurt?

9
Work
and
business

Business success

DOT.COM SUCCESS

Two young entrepreneurs, who started a new Internet business two years ago, have today sold the business for £3 million. Jenny Curtis, co-founder of Slimmm.com, says, 'Everyone thinks we've **made a killing**, but it was hard work. For the first 18 months we couldn't **make ends meet** - I couldn't even buy a new pair of socks! When the business finally **got off the ground**, we worked 18 hours a day for six months.'

---

make a killing
make a big profit quickly

make ends meet
have enough money to pay for necessities

get off the ground
start to be successful

*Joe **made a killing** when the spider-men visited Earth.*

Job interviews

Interviewers always ask difficult questions that nobody could possibly answer **off the cuff**. So it's important to be prepared for them.

But you can't prepare for everything, so sometimes you just have to **think on your feet**. Don't worry if you make a few mistakes.

Just remember what the psychologists tell us: most interviewers **make up their minds** in the first 30 seconds anyway.

off the cuff
without preparation

think on your feet
think as you go along

make up your mind
make a definite decision

*Most interviewers **make up their minds***
in the first 30 seconds.

In the red

B.I.G. in the red

Profits are down this year for the multinational B.I.G Co, and figures show the company is **in the red**. B.I.G.'s chief executive says, 'A slowdown in the world economy means that a lot of companies are **feeling the pinch**. Many are cutting their expenses and trying to operate **on a shoestring**, but we're big enough to keep going normally, and we'll be back **in the black** next year.'

---

in the red/black
in debt/credit

feel the pinch
begin to feel poor

on a shoestring
with little money to spend

*I know we're **on a shoestring**,*
but this is crazy!

A new job

When you start a new job, it takes some time before you feel confident about what to do and how to do it.

Ideally, an employer recognises this and allows you to **find your feet** before taking on anything too difficult.

But life is not always ideal, so you may be thrown **in at the deep end** and then you have to **sink or swim**.

find your feet
get used to a new situation

in at the deep end
directly into a difficult situation

sink or swim
survive (or not) without help

*On her first day, the new gardener was still **finding her feet**.*

Big fish

When Herman came to Britain to work,
he spoke good English but didn't know
many idioms. One day at work someone
said, 'Don't disturb the manager. She's
meeting some **big fish** from New York.'

'Big fish?' Herman asked.

'Yes, she's got a new project and she
wants to get them **on board**.'

As Herman reached for his dictionary of
English idioms, an extraordinary picture
formed in his **mind's eye**.

big fish
important influential people

on board
actively involved (The non-idiomatic
meaning is on a boat, bus, train or plane)

mind's eye
imagination

*She's trying to get some **big fish
on board**.*

Review 9

A Match the idioms and meanings.

1 off the cuff   a) imagination

2 in the red   b) without preparation

3 big fish   c) owing money

4 mind's eye   d) important person

B Complete the idioms.

1 I must choose, but I can't make up .... .

2 He started the business at home on a ....

3 It takes a few days to find your .... in a new job.

4 My salary is very low, and I can't make .... meet.

C Are these things good or bad for a business?

1 being in the black

2 feeling the pinch

3 making a killing

114

D Look at pictures 1 and 2 and complete the idioms.

1

You've had the training. Now you have to .... or swim.

2

The new business got .... quickly.

10

That's bad!

Bad things

We often use idioms when we react to bad things. For example, **'That's below the belt'** means someone has said something unfair and cruel in an argument. Idioms can also show that a speaker does not like something: 'Bob's **sitting on the fence'** means Bob is refusing to give an opinion, which is not necessarily bad, but the speaker thinks it's annoying.

Some idioms are direct and impolite, such as **'Mind your own business!'** which means 'This is private. Keep your nose out of it.'

below the belt
unfair and cruel

sit on the fence
be neutral

mind your own business
this is private

Mind your own business!

Bad or not?

Your employer says you must finish some work by tomorrow. Is it OK to cut corners, or would you work around the clock to do the work properly?

What would you do if somebody offered to pull strings to help you get into a good university or to get a good job?

What if a friend of yours commits a crime? Would you tell the police or turn a blind eye?

cut corners
do incomplete work

around the clock
for 24 hours a day

pull strings
use influential friends

turn a blind eye
ignore it

*The builders **cut corners**?*
What do you mean? It
looks great to me

Poison

Winston Churchill was famous for, amongst other things, his quick wit. On one occasion in parliament, the opposition party was **up in arms** because Churchill's government had given the **thumbs down** to a proposed new law.

The debate began to **get out of hand** and a woman shouted, 'If I were your wife, I'd give you poison.'

Churchill instantly replied, 'If you were my wife, I would drink it.'

up in arms
protesting strongly

thumbs down
negative response

(get) out of hand
(get) out of control

*The debate began to **get out of hand**.*

Embarrassing!

I was working as a tour guide and I was having a difficult time with a group of elderly ladies. None of my attempts to **break the ice** were working, and all my usual jokes were **falling flat**. I didn't know what to do to cheer them up.

A bit later I was getting out of the bus and I tripped and fell and tore my trousers. The ladies almost **split their sides**, and after that, everything was fine!

break the ice
create a relaxed atmosphere

fall flat
fail to have the desired effect

split their sides
laughed uncontrollably

*All his usual jokes **fell flat**.*

Kiss and tell

Government hit by scandal

The latest disaster for the government is the **kiss-and-tell** story in yesterday's *Sunday World* newspaper, in which a well-known actress told of her two-year affair with the Minister for the Family. As the man who **calls the shots** in the government's policy on family values, it seems certain that the Minister's **days are numbered**, and the government's credibility has been damaged.

kiss-and-tell
publicly telling the details of a love affair

calls the shots
is the decision maker

days are numbered
won't survive for much longer

*He knew his **days were numbered**.*

Review 10

A Match the idioms and meanings.

1 below the belt   a) ignore it
2 up in arms   b) unfair, cruel
3 turn a blind eye   c) protesting
4 fall flat   d) fail to amuse

B Complete the idioms.

1 Powerful people can get things by pulling .... .
2 The plan got the thumbs .... from the director, so it's going ahead.
3 The country has a king, but he doesn't call .... .
4 A friendly greeting helps to break .... .

C Do *you* -

1 express opinions or sit on the fence?
2 gossip or mind your own business?
3 cut corners sometimes?
4 ever work around the clock?

D Look at pictures 1 and 2 and complete the idioms.

1

They laughed so much, they almost ....
their sides.

2

By 6 pm, the children's party was getting ....

Idioms
List

An alphabetical list
of the idioms in this book
with an example for each idiom

around the clock
This airport is open around the clock.

at each other's throats
What's that noise? Are they at each other's throats again?

below the belt
I know you were angry, but that comment was below the belt.

be there for
My parents are great. They've always been there for me.

big fish
He's a big fish now that his company's successful.

break someone's heart
Losing him broke her heart.

break the ice
He told a joke to break the ice at the beginning of his speech.

breath of fresh air
In an office full of boring people, she was like a breath of fresh air.

burst out laughing
He looked angry, but suddenly burst out laughing.

by the book
The police can't do whatever they want; they have to go by the book.

call the shots
Britain lost her empire long ago and no longer calls the shots.

carry weight
He is an expert, so his opinions carry a lot of weight.

catch someone red handed
The police caught him red handed inside the bank at midnight.

couch potato
Couch potatoes, who don't use their minds or bodies, risk ill health.

cut corners
We'll have to cut corners if we're going to finish the job in time.

cut no ice
I thought I had a good excuse, but it cut no ice with my boss.

dark horse
The new director is a dark horse. I wonder what he's like.

days are numbered
When the lion came towards him, he thought his days were numbered.

dirty word
Love became a dirty word during the Chinese cultural revolution.

do the trick
This medicine should do the trick.

drop-dead gorgeous
He's not just good-looking, he's drop-dead gorgeous.

fall flat
It's embarrassing if a joke falls flat.

feel the pinch
Sales are down and the company is feeling the pinch.

find your feet
It takes some time to find your feet in a new situation.

fingers crossed
Let's keep our fingers crossed that the weather will be good.

fish out of water
I'm like a fish out of water in my new job.

from scratch
We'll have to start again from scratch.

full of yourself
She's too full of herself to be interested in other people.

get a life
Why don't you do something exciting? Get a life!

get it straight
Let's get this straight. I'm in charge here.
You follow me.

get off the ground
If we can get this idea off the ground,
we'll be rich.

get out of hand
The demonstration got out of hand and
twenty people were injured.

get the hang of
Keep practising and you'll soon get the
hang of it.

get your act together
I must get my act together and find a
good job.

give and take
If you want an agreement, you have to
accept some give and take.

the gloves are off
The gloves are off in the price war
between the two supermarkets.

go Dutch
He offered to pay for the meal, but we
had all agreed to go Dutch.

going steady
She's been going steady with her
boyfriend for a year.

go to the wall
Supermarkets are everywhere, and village
shops have gone to the wall.

golden rule
The golden rule of healthy exercise is not
to overdo it.

have a go
You might not enjoy it, but it's worth
having a go at it and finding out.

have a soft spot for
I have a soft spot for my little niece.

have a thing about
I've had a thing about her for years.

have someone on
You're not really a police officer, are you? You're having me on.

head over heels
She met him on holiday and fell head over heels for him.

he's/she's history
She used to go out with him, but he's history now.

hit it off
Mothers don't always hit it off with their son's girlfriends.

hit the nail on the head
A: This wine tastes like a Bordeaux.
B: You've hit the nail on the head. That's exactly what it is.

hot water
His extreme opinions are always getting him into hot water.

in at the deep end
There was a crisis on my first day, so I was thrown in at the deep end.

138

in stitches

The speaker was so funny that the audience were in stitches.

in the flesh

I've seen him on TV, but not in the flesh.

in the red/black

I spent a lot last month and now I'm in the red.

in the same boat

I understand your problem because you and I are in the same boat.

in the thick of

He was in the thick of the fighting, but was not injured.

In your dreams.

'Can I borrow your motorcycle?' - 'In your dreams.'

in your shoes

How would you feel if you were in my shoes?

just like that
I asked her and she said yes - just like that!

keep your head above water
The job is difficult, but I'm keeping my head above water.

keep a straight face
I wanted to laugh, but I managed to keep a straight face.

kick yourself
He kicked himself for forgetting her birthday.

kiss-and-tell
It is a kiss-and-tell book about her affair with the President.

larger than life
The characters in books and films are often larger than life.

leaves me cold
Everyone says it's a great film, but it left me cold.

let the cat out of the bag
The newspaper let the cat out of the bag
before the president's speech.

life in the fast lane
Life in the fast lane is exciting but tiring.

lost for words
The news was so unexpected that he was
lost for words.

lost it
Finally, he lost it and threw the computer
out of the window.

love at first sight
Their eyes met and it was love at first
sight.

make a killing
Umbrella shops make a killing in wet
weather.

make ends meet
I can't make ends meet on my very low
income.

make head nor tail of
I can't make head nor tail of this computer handbook.

make up your mind
You've looked at 12 pairs of shoes. It's time to make up your mind!

mind's eye
In my mind's eye I'm on a beach in Barbados.

mind your own business
'How much do you earn?' - 'Mind your own business.'

miss the boat
She wanted to have children and was afraid of missing the boat.

Mr Right
'Will I ever find my Mr Right?' she wondered.

no rocket scientist
He can't understand the instructions - he's no rocket scientist.

no way
'Do you think they could win? - 'No way.'

off the cuff
I can't answer that question off the cuff.

off the hook
He got off the hook because the police lost the evidence.

on a roll
The company is on a roll. All their new products have done well.

on a shoestring
He started the business on a shoestring, working at home.

on board
He's starting a new company and he wants me on board.

on cloud nine
When she agreed to marry him, he was on cloud nine.

on Earth
Where on Earth were you? What on Earth are you doing?

on edge
I'm always a bit on edge before an important meeting.

only have eyes for
I'm not interested in him - I only have eyes for you.

on me
Put your money away. The drinks are on me.

on the cards
We can't be sure that it'll happen, but it's on the cards.

on the go
You're always on the go. You should relax sometimes.

on the line
Fire officers sometimes put their lives on the line to save others.

on top of
We've had problems but we're getting on top of them now.

on top of the world
Yesterday I was on top of the world, but today I feel miserable.

get out of hand
The demonstration got out of hand and twenty people were injured.

over the moon
That's wonderful news! You must be over the moon about it.

pain in the neck
My little brother can be a pain in the neck.

party pooper
I'm sorry to be a party pooper, but I don't want to play this game.

pick up the pieces
After a very bad year, we're picking up the pieces.

pick up the tab
The taxpayer has to pick up the tab for the government's mistakes.

piece of cake
The test was a piece of cake. I got 100%.

play hard to get
Don't you like him or are you playing hard to get?

play it by ear
We don't know what will happen, so we'll have to play it by ear.

pop the question
He pulled out a ring and popped the question.

pull someone's leg
It's not really true. I'm just pulling your leg.

pull strings
He has important friends and can pull strings to get what he wants.

pull the other one
Pull the other one. I know that's not true.

push the boat out
People usually push the boat out when they get married.

put your feet up
When I've finished this work, I can put my feet up.

put your foot in it
I'm sorry. I've put my foot in it. I didn't want to upset you.

rat race
She dropped out of the rat race to become an artist.

safe bet
It's a safe bet that we won't win the Cup.

score an own goal
The company scored an own goal by angering environmentalists.

see eye to eye

We don't see eye to eye on politics so we try to avoid the subject.

see red

During an argument, she saw red and attacked him with a knife.

sink or swim

They gave me some training and then left me to sink or swim.

sit on the fence

If we sit on the fence, the bad guys might win.

slip your mind

I'm sorry. Your birthday just slipped my mind.

small talk

I don't like parties where I don't know anyone - I'm not good at small talk.

soft touch

I know I'm a soft touch. I just can't say 'No' to people.

spill the beans
Don't tell her, because she'll spill the
beans to everybody.

split their sides
The film was so funny the audience were
splitting their sides.

step on it
Step on it! We're late!

sweep someone off their feet
He swept her off her feet. And now
they're married.

take a rain check
Thanks. I can't come tonight, but can I
take a rain check?

take some doing
It'll take some doing to carry that piano
upstairs.

take to heart
He took the doctor's advice to heart and
stopped smoking.

take your time
Take your time. There's no hurry.

That would be telling.
We could give you the answer, but that would be telling.

that'll be the day
A: Is your brother married?
B: That'll be the day!

the gloves are off
The gloves are off in the price war between the two supermarkets.

the man in the street
The man in the street wants a change of government.

think on your feet
A soldier has to think on his feet.

at each other's throats
What's that noise? Are they at each other's throats again?

thumbs down
The government has given the thumbs down to a tax cut.

tie the knot
After living together for three years, they decided to tie the knot.

to death
What a terrible film. I was bored to death.

to say the least
Skydiving is not the safest sport, to say the least.

touch and go
We won in the end, but it was touch and go until the last minute.

touch base
Touch base with the police and find out if they've discovered anything.

turn a blind eye
Although it's illegal, the police often turn a blind eye to it.

turn heads

It's a fast, stylish car that turns heads.

turn the tables

He managed to get the gun and turn the tables on the robber.

two-timing

She's two-timing him. She's seeing someone else too.

up in arms

Lorry drivers are up in arms about the cost of fuel.

what got into him

I've never seen him so angry! What got into him?

You can say *that* again.

A: It's cold, isn't it?

B: You can say that again.

You're telling *me*.

A: This hotel is terrible.

B: You're telling me.

Answers – Review 1

A 1 larger than life = b) exciting
    2 dark horse = a) obscure person
    3 on the go = c) active, busy

B 1 She was so surprised that she was lost for words.
    2 He's too full of himself to be interested in us.
    3 My little brother can be a pain in the neck.
    4 The man in the street cares more about money than politics.

Answers – Review 2

A 1 on edge = c) anxious
    2 in stitches = a) laughing a lot
    3 lose it = d) be out of control
    4 see red = b) feel very angry

B 1 I feel on top of the world when the sun shines.
    2 She burst out laughing when she saw me.
    3 I'm on cloud nine whenever we're together.
    4 He suddenly hit me. I don't know what got into him.

Answers – Review 3

A 1 see eye to eye = d) agree
  2 it's on me = c) I'll pay
  3 hit it off = a) like each other
  4 fingers crossed = b) Let's hope
B 1 The nice new secretary was a breath of fresh air.
  2 You paid last time. This meal is on me.
  3 I think he has a soft spot for you.
  4 Thanks, but I can't come tonight. Can I take a rain check?
  5 Give and take is important in a good relationship.

Answers – Review 4

A 1 no way = b) definitely not
  2 go steady = c) in a regular relationship
  3 he's history = d) in the past
  4 go Dutch = a) share costs
B 1 As soon as they met, it was love at first sight.
  2 He took out a ring and popped the question.
  3 Some people plan, others play it by ear.
  4 He's in love and only has eyes for her.
D 1 In your dreams!
  2 … has a thing about ponytails.

Answers – Review 5

A 1 Mr Right = c) the ideal husband
   2 hot water = b) trouble
   3 put your feet up = a) relax
   4 off the hook = d) out of trouble

B 1 We're in the same boat, so let's help each other.
   2 You need to get your act together and find a job.
   3 He left the rat race to do charity work.
   4 How would you feel if you were in my shoes?

C 2, feeling like a fish out of water

Answers – Review 6

A 1 two-time = b) be unfaithful
   2 spill the beans = a) reveal a secret
   3 You're telling *me*. = d) I know that already and I agree
   4 pulling my leg = c) teasing me

B 1 Pull the other one.
   2 That would be telling.
   3 You can say *that* again.
   4 Yes. You've hit the nail on the head.

Answers – Review 7

A 1 touch and go = a) unsure
   2 on the cards = d) likely
   3 tie the knot = b) get married
   4 have a go = c) try

B 1 We'll have to start again from scratch.
   2 Some people can memorise phrases just
      like that.
   3 A golden rule of learning is to practise
      regularly.
   4 It's a safe bet that I'll forget …
   5 … but now I'm getting the hang of it.

C 1 That'll be the day!
   2 … but it cut no ice with him at all.

Answers – Review 8

A 1 piece of cake = b) easy
   2 take your time = c) don't hurry
   3 step on it = a) go faster
   4 miss the boat = d) be too late

B 1 The police caught the thief red handed.
   2 The campaign has started, and the
      gloves are off.
   3 We made a mistake and scored an own
      goal.
   4 The doctor said, 'These pills will do the
      trick.'

Answers – Review 9

A 1 off the cuff = b) without preparation
   2 in the red = c) owing money
   3 big fish = d) important person
   4 mind's eye = a) imagination
B 1 … I can't make up my mind.
   2 … at home on a shoestring.
   3 … to find your feet in a new job.
   4 … and I can't make ends meet.
C 1 good 2 bad 3 good
D 1 sink or swim 2 got off the ground

Answers – Review 10

A 1 below the belt = b) unfair, cruel
   2 up in arms = c) protesting
   3 turn a blind eye = a) ignore it
   4 fall flat = d) fail to amuse
B 1 … get things by pulling strings.
   2 The plan got the thumbs up
   3 … but he doesn't call the shots.
   4 … helps to break the ice.
D 1 … they almost split their sides.
   2 … was getting out of hand.

Printed in Poland
by Amazon Fulfillment
Poland Sp. z o.o., Wrocła